SPIRIT OF
NORWICH

DANIEL TINK

First published in Great Britain in 2010

British Library Cataloguing-in-Publication Data
A CIP record for this title is available from the British Library

ISBN 978 1 906887 99 5

PiXZ Books
Halsgrove House, Ryelands Industrial Estate,
Bagley Road, Wellington, Somerset TA21 9PZ
Tel: 01823 653777
Fax: 01823 216796
email: sales@halsgrove.com

An imprint of Halstar Ltd, part of the Halsgrove group of companies
Information on all Halsgrove titles is available at: www.halsgrove.com

Printed and bound in China by Toppan Leefung Printing Ltd

Introduction

Set in the heart of beautiful Norfolk, the fine city of Norwich is a fascinating blend of old and new, with a bustling commercial centre.

Charming cobbled streets include the famous Elm Hill with its picturesque Tudor architecture and the popular Norwich Lanes with its vibrant mix of independent shops. Standing proud the magnificent castle sits on its great mound housing fine collections of art and history. Add two beautiful cathedrals and a host of elegant churches contained within the ancient city walls, and you have vivid picture of Norwich's historic past.

The city offers a generous supply of restaurants, cafés and pubs with tastes and flavours for all to enjoy. Shoppers have the choice of two malls, a colourful marketplace and access to all the modern city amenities. Beautiful parks and gardens provide peaceful recreation and delightful places to explore.

The photographs in this book have been selected to provide a glimpse of much of the best that this exciting city has to offer.

Daniel Tink

Norwich Castle was built around the year 1100 on the instructions of William the Conqueror, to replace a Norman timber castle keep. Steeped in history it stands at over 70 feet in height, and has had many uses in the past including a royal palace, a gaol, and more recently a museum showcasing historic artifacts and fabulous art galleries.

Opposite:
Battlement tours at Norwich Castle provide stunning views over the city. With a guide explaining some of the history and facts of the city, this makes a fascinating experience. The short series of photos that follow show some of the different views from all sides of the castle.

Norwich City Hall is an art deco building that was completed in 1938 and opened by King George VI and Queen Elizabeth. The Roman Catholic Cathedral can be seen in the background.

The magnificent St Peter Mancroft church (often mistaken for being the city's cathedral) stands opposite to, and in stark contrast to, the modern architecture of the Forum.

Left:
A view of east Norwich from the battlements of Norwich Castle. If you look carefully you will spot the Train Station, Lady Julian Bridge at Riverside and Norwich City Football Club Stadium.

Looking towards Riverside from the Novi Sad Friendship Bridge. A peaceful stroll along the River Wensum takes you past the Riverside complex, where you'll find a refreshing variety of bars and the latest addition to the wide range of bridges in Norwich, the Lady Julian Bridge.

Novi Sad Friendship Bridge was opened in 2001 and celebrates the close connection between Norwich and Novi Sad, our twin town in Serbia.

Lady Julian Bridge was opened in 2009 and is named after the famous mystic, Julian of Norwich. The bridge provides a new link between Riverside and the city centre.

The view from Lady Julian Bridge, looking towards the Novi Sad Friendship Bridge.

Norwich railway station was opened in the nineteenth century.
At one time there were three railway stations in Norwich!

Right:
A short walk from the railway station brings you to the River Wensum that meanders around the north and east sides of the city centre. It has beautiful riverside walks and seasonal boat cruises, with views of Norwich Cathedral and Cow Tower.

Pull's Ferry is a flint building, once used as a medieval watergate. Monks built a canal from the River Wensum along which stone was transported for building the cathedral. The cathedral spire is visible in the background.

Norwich Cathedral on a cold morning after snowfall. Taken at sunrise, the spire shows the warm glow of the sun.

Norwich Cathedral was completed in the twelfth century and is built from limestone brought in from Caen, France. The spire is the second tallest in England and was originally made from wood. This did not fare well in strong storms and was rebuilt several times before the stone spire seen today was constructed in the late fifteenth century.

The Duke of Wellington statue in the attractive grounds of Norwich Cathedral.

Erpingham Gate was built around 1420 by Sir Thomas Erpingham, an English Knight who led King Henry V's archers at the Battle of Agincourt in 1415. The gate provides access to Norwich Cathedral from Tombland.

Ethelbert Gate is the second gateway to Norwich Cathedral from Tombland and was built by the citizens of Norwich after the original gate was destroyed during a riot.

In Tombland, and located next to Norwich Cathedral, the Maids Head Hotel is one of the city's most historic hostelrys.

Tombland is neighbour to Norwich Cathedral and was once the setting for a Saxon market place. It is now rich with restaurants and bars and despite its grim sounding name, Tombland actually translates to "open space". It is reported to be the most haunted part of Norwich.

The narrow Tombland Alley links Tombland with Princes Street and runs adjacent to the church of St George Tombland. The leaning building above the archway dates back to 1530 and was built by the cloth merchant, Augustine Steward.

The cobbled Princes Street is a mix of old and new on either side. The pretty church of St George Tombland completes this picturesque scene.

Not far from Princes Street is an historic cobbled lane with buildings dating back to Tudor times. This is the famous Elm Hill, which once narrowly escaped plans for demolition.

Take your time to stroll down pretty Elm Hill, visiting the numerous antique shops and art galleries, or have a cuddle with the toy bears of the Bear Shop.

Opposite:
This view from Fye Bridge shows the River Wensum and Quay Side. Like many vantage points in Norwich, the Cathedral spire can be seen in the skyline.

A view of the River Wensum taken from Whitefriars Bridge. The City Hall clock can be seen towering in the distance.

The River Wensum and Whitefriars Bridge. Built in the 1920s, it replaced the original one of 1591.

Cow Tower next to the River Wensum is a symbolic reminder of Norwich's medieval past, with its name deriving from grazing cattle that used it as shelter.

In the fourteenth century Norwich had completed construction of its city walls, around two-and-a-half miles in length. Built to keep the enemy out, much of the remains, including towers, can still be found in today's modern city. The Black Tower (pictured) is located at Carrow Hill.

The Adam and Eve pub is believed to be the oldest alehouse in Norwich dating back to 1249 when it was first registered as a public house. The saying goes that Norwich once had a pub for every day of the year. Today, Norwich still has a great selection of varied pubs and bars.

Built in 1340, Bishop Bridge is the last remaining medieval bridge in Norwich.

Opposite:
A cruise boat near Fye Bridge picks up more passengers for a trip along the River Wensum.

The River Wensum flows past the Norwich School of Art and under Blackfriars Bridge (also known as St George's Bridge), built in 1783.

Opposite:
St George's Street offers a range of entertainment, from an Irish themed bar to the playhouse theatre. You will also find the attractive St Andrew's and Blackfriars' Halls.

GUINNESS
DELANEYS IRISH

Norwich Lanes is the name given to the numerous cobbled walkways and streets which are home to quaint independent shops full of charm and character. It makes for a great place to visit and an ideal escape from the busy high streets.

Right and opposite: St Gregory's Green, in the heart of Norwich Lanes, is a small but pleasant place to sit and relax. Once a year it plays host to a colourful array of stalls and events to celebrate the Norwich Lanes midsummer fair.

DON PEPÉ
RESTAURANT
NORWICH
633979
Arnolds
TO LET

St Benedict's Street enjoys a festival atmosphere every summer when a variety of entertainment brings fun and laughter, and stalls flood the street with colour.

Pottergate is said to have once been the home of medieval pot makers. It is now a popular street in the Norwich Lanes that leads to the pleasant St Gregory's Green where benches provide a welcome rest.

Lobster Lane leading to Bedford Street. Lobster Lane was dramatically shortened in 1883 when it was divided into two parts; Lobster Lane and Bedford Street.

The swan in Swan Lane at Christmas. Look up or you might miss it!

BrambleS!
THORNS
THORNS
THORNS
THORNS
IRONMONGERS & TOOL MERCHANTS
SECURITY GARDEN & HOME CENTRE

Above left: Lower Goat Lane in the Norwich Lanes, offers a colourful mixture of small unique shops. The City Hall clock tower dominates the skyline looking up the lane.

Above right: This cafe in Lower Goat Lane is one of an abundance of cafes, restaurants and pubs to be found in Norwich, each bringing their own styles and tastes.

Opposite: Exchange Street is home to the famous family run Jarrold's department store and delightful shops and restaurants of the Norwich Lanes.

Above: Busy shoppers in the historic London Street. Once named Cockey Lane, London Street was introduced as the new name in 1828, it is said because it reminded people of the busy streets of London.

Right: Norwich Guildhall was built in the fifteenth century and has been a host to court rooms, prisoners and more recently, tourists.

Morris dancing in Gentleman's Walk. Street entertainment and buskers are often found in Gentleman's Walk, which is also home to a colourful and friendly market – the largest open air market in England!

BANK LIMITED

Left:
Christmas lights beautifully illuminate the market and Gentleman's Walk.

Between Gentleman's Walk and Castle Street you will find the Royal Arcade designed by George Skipper in 1899. Arcades like this were the forerunners of today's shopping malls. Inside you will find delightful little shops amongst the beautiful architecture.

Gentleman's Walk is packed with high street names and the thousands of daily shoppers that use them. The name Gentleman's Walk originates from the gentleman of the eighteenth century who used the area for their daily adventures, which more than often involved drinking in the many inns in the area.

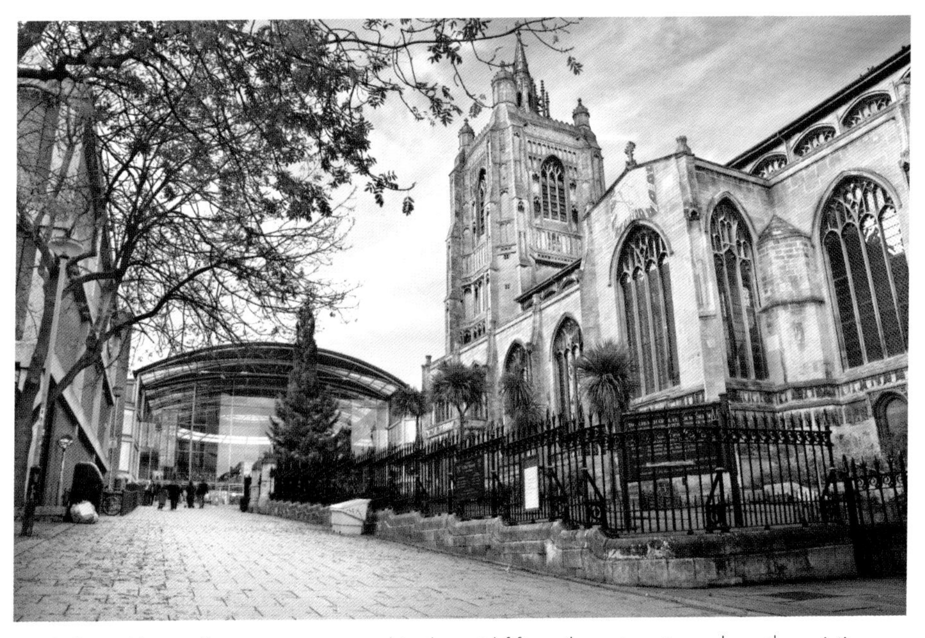

St Peter Mancroft was reconstructed in the mid fifteenth century to replace the existing church that dated back to the eleventh century. The Forum can be seen in the background.

The Forum is a £65 million pound building built on the site of the former Library, which was sadly destroyed by fire in 1994. Today the Forum is home to not only the library, but also a café, bar and restaurant, a tourist information centre, an art and gift shop, and also hosts regular exhibitions. The Forum is a truly wonderful experience where you can easily lose all track of time!

Below: There are several areas in Norwich that were used when markets were flourishing and specialised areas grew. A popular market was timber, which is how the name Timberhill was introduced to this street.

BELL HOTEL.
YORK HOUSE
BAKERS OVEN
SHOP TO LET
BUSES ONLY

Left:
Castle Meadow leading to Red Lion Street, seen from Norwich Castle. A walk around the walls of the castle provides fantastic views of the surrounding city.

Built in the early twentieth century, the elegant Surrey House on Surrey Street was the headquarters of Norwich Union, now known as Aviva.

Norwich Bus Station on Surrey Street is a 5 million pound development built in 2005 to replace the old station. Its distinctive design is impressive to look at and has become yet another famous landmark in Norwich.

St Stephen's Street is home to many high street stores and provides access to Chapelfield shopping complex.

Left:
The famous Norwich Union clock became part of Surrey Street in 1927.

St Stephen's roundabout.

Opposite: Norwich is proud to boast two cathedrals. St John the Baptist Roman Catholic Cathedral was constructed between 1882 and 1910 and is an incredible sight up close; it is particularly spectacular illuminated at night.

The Roman Catholic Cathedral of St John the Baptist provides weekend tower tours for those with a good head for heights. After a spiral staircase climb you'll find yourself at the highest point in Norwich with spectacular views of the city. On a clear day with a pair of binoculars you can see Happisburgh Lighthouse, roughly twenty miles distant.

Opposite:
A view from the Roman Catholic Cathedral tower, looking towards the green trees of Chapelfield Gardens, City Hall, the Forum and miles of surrounding landscape beyond the city.

Chapelfield Gardens is a peaceful green area that neighbours the Chapelfield shopping complex. It provides the perfect place to relax after a busy shopping trip, or to take the family on a picnic where you might be fortunate to hear a brass band playing in the band stand!

Following the First World War, funds were made available to develop parks as a means of allowing the public to relax and forget about worries of unemployment and tribulation. Heigham Park was one such park and today has plenty to offer all the family.

Wensum Park on the north of the city was opened in 1925 and lies beside the River Wensum. Wensum Park is a wonderful place to visit, with tranquil walks along the river, activities for children and scenic picnic areas.

Eaton Park is the largest of all Norwich parks and was opened in 1928 by the Princess of Wales. The park has something for everyone including sporting and leisure activities.

The University of East Anglia – the first students arrived in 1963 – lies roughly three miles west of the city centre. The grounds near the campus are popular amongst students and walkers, with wonderful countryside walks in the River Yare Valley. It also attracts fishermen, thanks to the university acquiring its own lake in the 1970s.

Opposite:
Colourful graffiti brings life to a wall on campus, at the University of East Anglia.

OBEY
OBEY
OBEY
OBEY
OBEY

Norwich City skyline from St James Hill, showing all major city landmarks including, from left to right: Norwich Castle, St Peter Mancroft, The Forum, City Hall, Norwich Cathedral and the Roman Catholic Cathedral.